SCHOLASTIC MATH PLACE™

REAL WORLD MATH FOR THINKING KIDS

Trash Plans

Using Math to Help Us Make Decisions About Our Environment

Published in cooperation with
The Conservation Fund
Arlington, Virginia

 Published by Scholastic Inc. Printed in U.S.A.
ISBN 0-590-27896-7
1 2 3 4 5 6 7 8 9 10 09 01 00 99 98 97 96 95 94

By planning, modeling, and reasoning, we optimize our decision making.

Trash Plans

We estimate and use mathematical operations, maps, and schedules to make decisions about our environment.

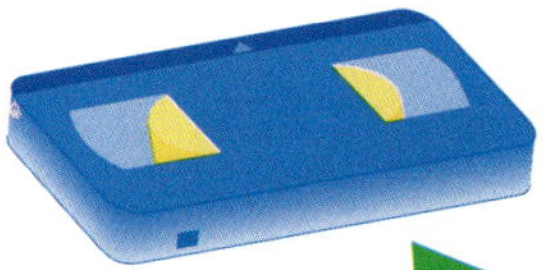

Video

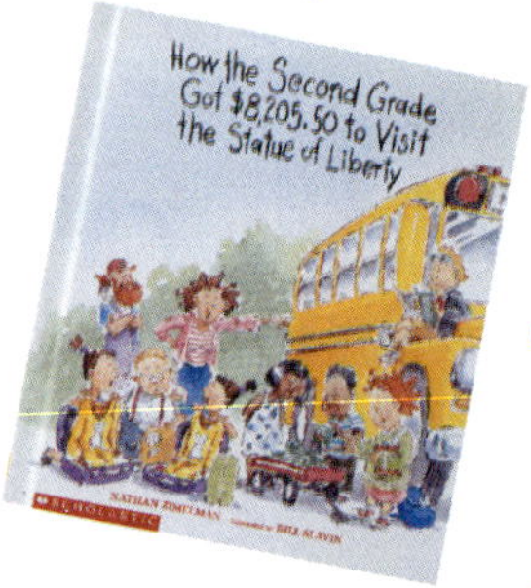

Big Book

SUBCONCEPT 1

We estimate area to manage our space.

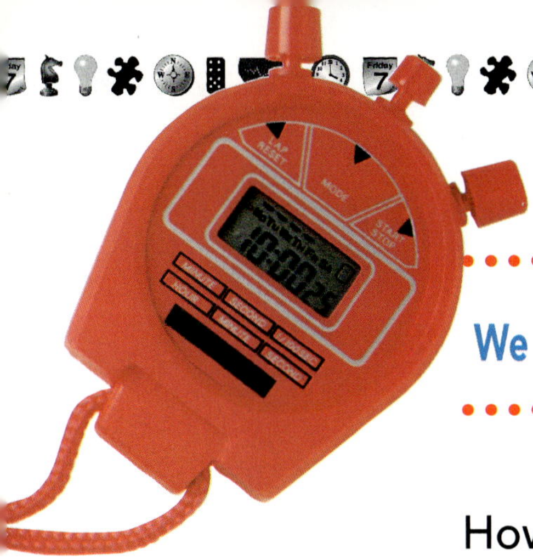

SUBCONCEPT 2

We add, subtract, and explore larger numbers to help us plan.

Read Aloud

SUBCONCEPT 3

We make maps and use schedules to help organize our activities.

What Kinds of Trash Does Your Class Make?

Do you ever think about the trash you make? What kinds of trash do you think you would find if you looked in your class wastebasket?

Sort your trash.

DO-IT

- Work as a class. Empty and sort the trash in your wastebasket.
- Make a class graph to show what you sorted.

SHARE-IT

- What kinds of trash did your class make?
- What is there the most of?
- How many are in each category?

BUILD-ON-IT

- Talk about how your class can make less trash. Then write about it.
- Work with your class. Start a paper collection to recycle.

THINK

How else can you sort your class's trash?

How Can You Measure the Trash Your Class Makes?

You can measure trash in different ways. You can weigh it. You can count the pieces. You can also find out how much trash it takes to fill a wastebasket.

Measure your trash.

DO·IT

- How much trash does your class make in 1 day? Measure the height of the trash in the wastebasket to find out.
- How can you use your measurement to predict how much trash your class would make in 2 days? 3 days?

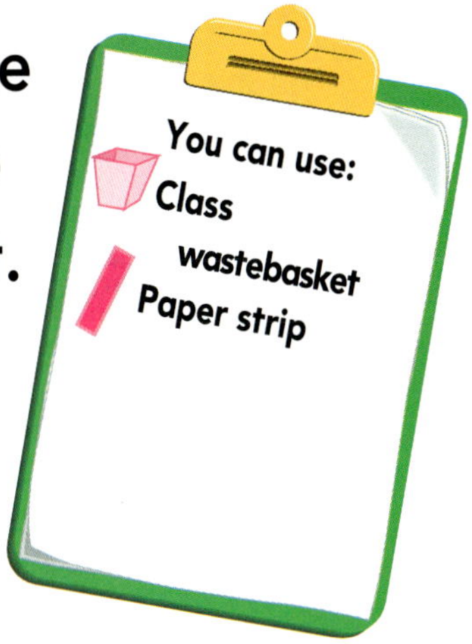

SHARE·IT

- Share how you measured and predicted.
- How many wastebaskets would your class fill in 1 week?

BUILD·ON·IT

- Predict how many wastebaskets all the second-grade classes would fill in 1 week.

THINK

How else can you measure trash?

Where Would You Put the Trash Your Class Makes?

What if your class had to store its trash in the classroom for a long time? Where would be a good place to store the trash?

Plan a trash center.

DO·IT

- Work with a partner. Decide where to store the trash.
- Make tracings of the bottom of your wastebasket.
- How many tracings will fit on the floor of your trash center?

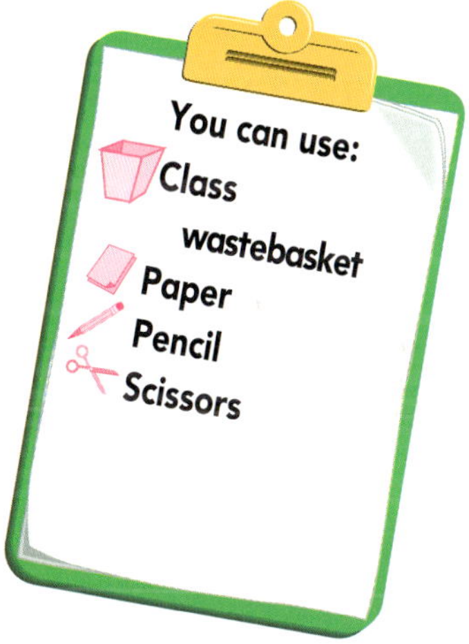

SHARE·IT

- Show and tell how you arranged the tracings.

BUILD·ON·IT

- How many tracings long is each side of your space?
- How many tracings in all fit in the space?

THINK

Is there another way to line up the tracings so that they cover the same area? Try it.

How Many Trash Centers Would Fit in Your Class?

What if you wanted to have more than one trash center?

You can use:
- Large sheet of paper
- Tape measure
- Pencil

Estimate.

DO·IT

- Work with a partner. Estimate how many trash centers would fit in your classroom.
- How could making a floor tracing help you find out how many would fit? How could measuring help you?

SHARE·IT

- Share what you did.
- Compare your estimate and your method with what others did.

BUILD·ON·IT

- How many wastebaskets would fit on the floor of your classroom?
- Tell how you figured it out.

THINK

How would you divide a pile of newspapers into smaller equal piles?

How Many Wastebaskets Would Fill Your Trash Center?

Can you imagine your trash center piled up high with wastebaskets? How many wastebaskets do you think this would be?

Find the volume.

DO·IT
- Make your trash center as high as your shoulders. How many wastebaskets would fit in this space?
- Make a cube model to help you.

SHARE·IT
- How many cubes did you put in one layer of your model?
- How many layers did you make?

BUILD·ON·IT
- Put together enough models to show all the trash centers that could fit in the classroom.
- Estimate the number of cubes in the class model.

You can use:
Classroom wastebasket
Snapcubes
Paper strip

THINK

How many school milk cartons do you think your wastebasket can hold?

When Would Your Trash Fill the Classroom?

What if your class fills 1 wastebasket of trash a day? How long would it take to fill your classroom with trash?

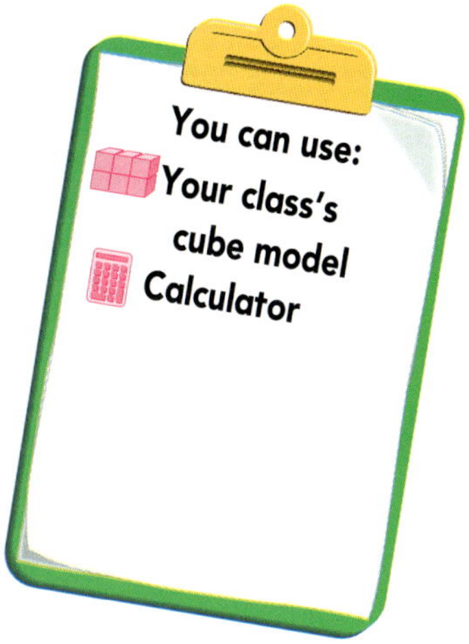

Find the length of time.

DO·IT

- Work with your class. Use the cube model your class put together.
- Count the cubes to find out how long it would take to fill the classroom with trash.
- Decide on the easiest way to count the cubes.

SHARE·IT

- Tell how you counted. What groups did you make?

BUILD·ON·IT

- Would it take longer or shorter than a year to fill your classroom with trash? Tell how you figured it out.

THINK

Why is it easier to skip-count by 5's than by 7's?

When Would the School's Trash Fill the Classroom?

Imagine that every wastebasket in your school is filled each day. How long would it take to fill your classroom with the school's trash?

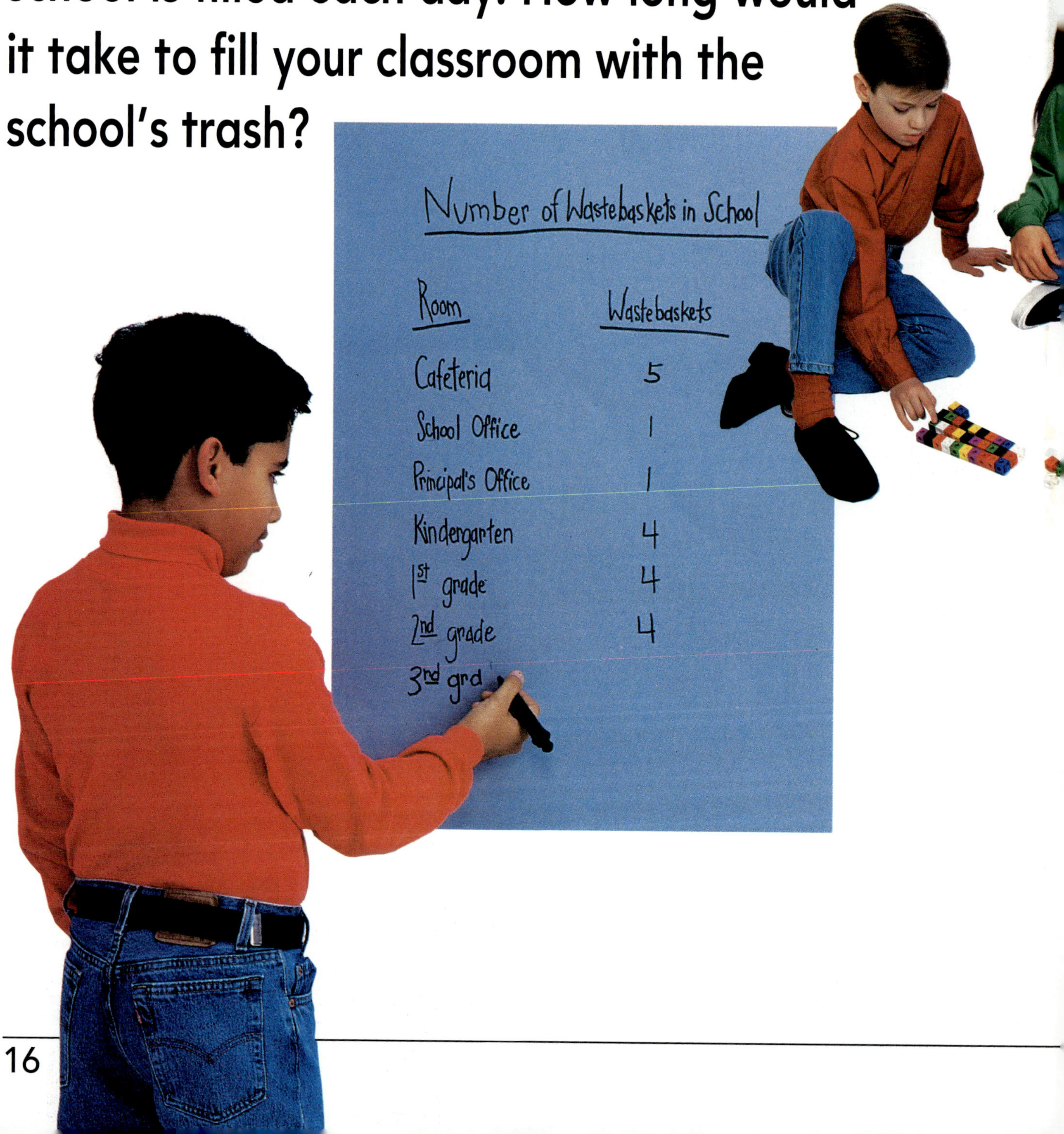

You can use:

- Snap cubes
- Paper
- Pencil
- Calendar
- Calculator

Mark the date.

DO·IT

- Work with your class. Find out how many wastebaskets are in your school.
- How many wastebaskets of trash would there be after 1 day? 2 days? 3 days?
- How long would it take to fill the classroom?

SHARE·IT

- Tell how you solved the problem.

BUILD·ON·IT

- On what date would the classroom be filled with the school's trash?

THINK

How much paper is in your paper collection now? How would you measure it?

How Many Trips Would It Take to Empty the Trash?

You have figured out how many wastebaskets of trash could fit in your classroom. How many trips would it take your class to empty this trash?

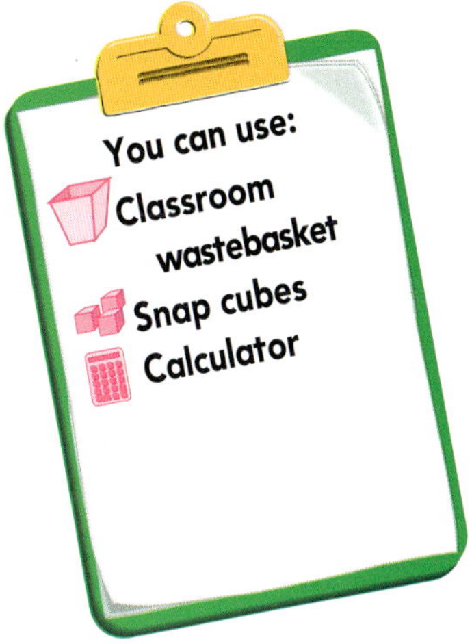

Make a plan.

DO·IT

- Pick up a wastebasket to see how heavy it is.
- Decide how many wastebaskets each kid could carry.
- How many wastebaskets would the class be able to move in one trip?

SHARE·IT

- Talk about how you made your decision.

BUILD·ON·IT

- Use cubes to figure out how many trips the class would have to make to empty the classroom.

THINK

How many trips in and out of the classroom does your class make?

Where Does Your School Keep Its Trash?

Do you know where your school stores its trash? How would you get there?

Find a path.

DO·IT

- Take a class walk to where your school stores its trash. What rooms do you pass? What corners do you turn?
- Estimate the number of steps before you leave your classroom. Count the steps as you walk back.

SHARE·IT

- Describe the path your class took.
- Compare the estimate you made to the actual number of steps.

BUILD·ON·IT

- What words did your class use to describe the path? Use them to describe a path in your classroom.

How Can You Make a Map?

What path did you take on your walk?
You can make a map to show the path.

Make a map.

You can use:
- Cubes
- Graph paper
- Tape
- Paper
- Pencil

DO·IT

- Work with a partner. Make a map of your walk.
- Put room numbers on the cubes.
- Take turns giving directions from your room to another room.

SHARE·IT • Use your map. What patterns do you see in the room numbers?

BUILD·ON·IT • Label your map with letters and numbers.

• Use them to describe where a room is.

THINK

What is the pattern of the addresses on the street where you live?

How Long Is the Trip to the School's Trash Area?

You know the way to the trash area in your school. How long does it take to get there?

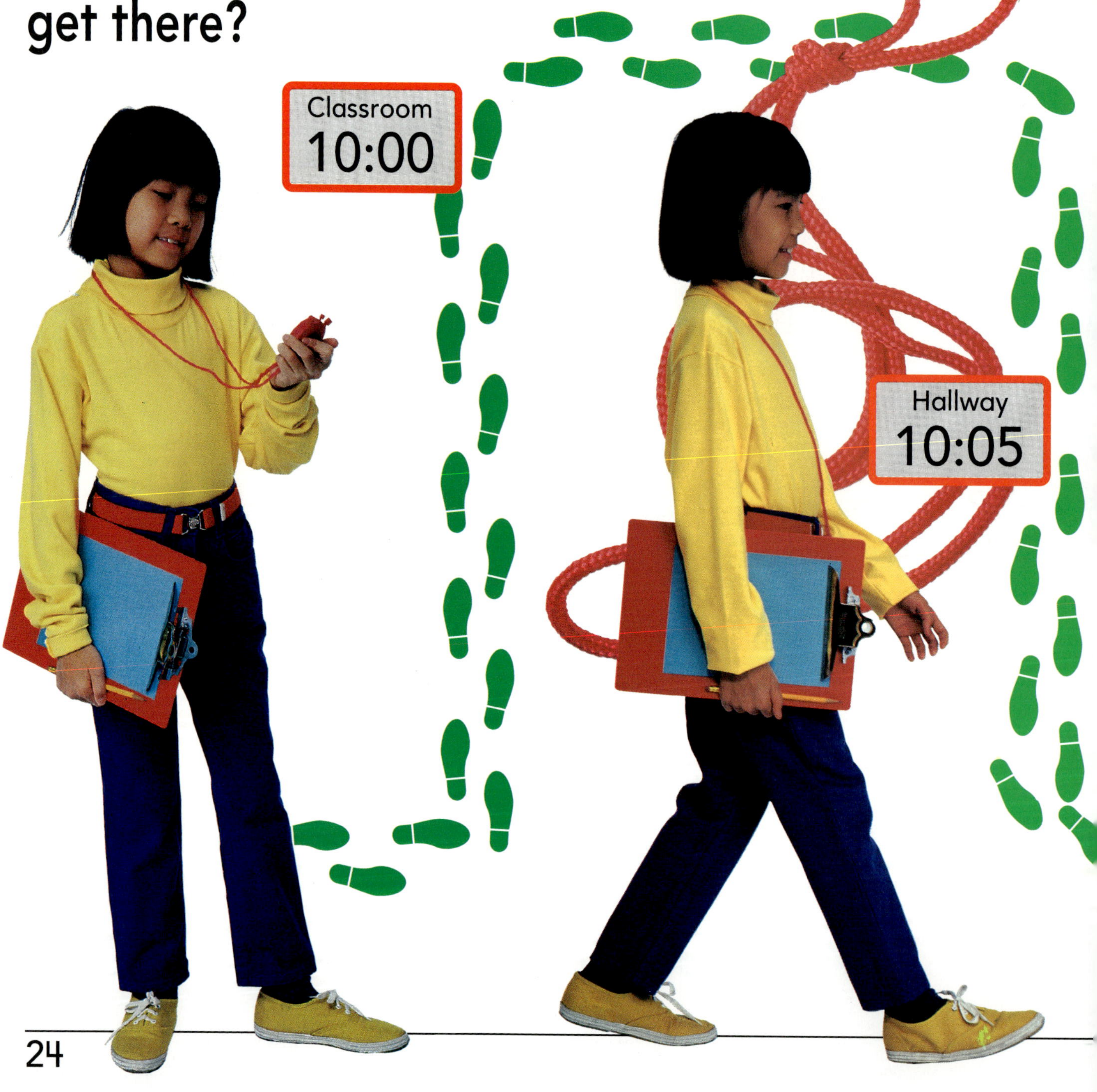

Time yourself.

DO·IT

- Work with your class. Start from your classroom. Find out how long it takes to get to your school's trash area and back to your classroom.
- Show the time you leave and return.

SHARE·IT

- How long did your trip take? Did it take more or less than half an hour? How long would 2 trips take? 3 trips? How did you find out?

BUILD·ON·IT

- What if you left your classroom at 10:30? What time would you return? Show the time on your clock.

What Is the Trash Pickup Schedule?

When does the garbage truck pick up garbage at your school? How can you be sure your paper collection will be at the school's trash area in time for the pickup?

Make a trash schedule.

You can use:
- Paper
- Pencil

DO·IT
- Work with a partner. Make a schedule to get your paper collection to the school's trash area in time for the pickup.
- Put a time next to each thing on your list.

SHARE·IT
- Use everyone's ideas to make a class trash schedule. Remember to allow time for the school custodian to put all the trash together.

BUILD·ON·IT
- Carry out the class plan. How would you do it differently the next time?

THINK

What patterns are there on a clock?

What Happens to the Trash During the Day?

Where does the trash go after it is picked up?

Watch the time.

You can use:
- Paper
- Pencil
- Clock stamp

DO·IT

- Where is the trash at 7 A.M.? 10 A.M.? 2 P.M.? 7 P.M.?
- What are you doing at those times?
- What other hours are there in a day?

- What hours are A.M. hours? P.M. hours?
- Why is it important to say A.M. or P.M. when you give the time?

THINK

What time do you think 13 o'clock is?

- Make a schedule of what you do in a 24-hour day.

When Do You Make Trash in School?

What is your school day like? When do you make trash during the school day?

Tell the time.

- Use your school schedule.
- During which activities do you make trash?
- What times are those activities? Show each time on a clock.

SHARE IT

- Share what you recorded.
- How much time is there between each activity?

BUILD ON IT

- What if you have to clean up $\frac{1}{4}$ hour before you go home? What time would you have to start cleaning up?

THINK

Why do you think the time 8:15 is also a quarter past 8?

What Can You Say About Your Classroom Trash?

Write a letter to a friend. Describe your favorite activity in this unit. Tell what you learned from it.